1862
FREDERICKSBURG
A New Look at a
Bitter Civil War Battle

by K. M. Kostyal

photography by Lori Epstein

NATIONAL GEOGRAPHIC
WASHINGTON, D.C.

CONTENTS

Dressed as a Union soldier, Greg Hillenbrand plays a tune on the fife during a reenactment of the 1862 Battle of Fredericksburg.

FOREWORD

OF ALL THE SOUTHERN TOWNS that went to war in 1861, few had the war come back upon them more violently, more completely, than did Fredericksburg, Virginia. Four times armies blue and gray clashed on the fields and farms in and around Fredericksburg, leaving a legacy of death and suffering unmatched anywhere on the continent. For 18 months the armies occupied, maneuvered, battled, or camped upon the landscape. They left behind a town devastated, homes ruined, farms scarred by miles of earthworks (still visible today), woodlots destroyed, lives forever altered, and places forever redefined.

War brought anguish, but also freedom. For the Fredericksburg region's 12,000 slaves (nearly half the population), the arrival of the Union Army in 1862 made freedom a real possibility. That spring and summer, as many as 10,000 slaves from surrounding counties—one man came from 62 miles away—poured into Union lines near Fredericksburg. Many of them crossed the Rappahannock River to freedom. Among them was Fredericksburg slave John Washington. "Life had a new joy awaiting me," he remembered.

Few towns in the United States have a history that reverberates beyond its boundaries, across the American landscape. Fredericksburg is one such place—the home of presidents, a place of import and sadness, and a setting for freedom gained.

—John Hennessy

Even children served in the Civil War, often as drummer boys. The sound of the fife and snare drum (right) kept armies marching forward.

INTRODUCTION

America in the mid-1800s was full of both promise and contradictions—the promise of freedom and prosperity for some and endless enslavement for others.

Since the founding of America, slavery had been an obvious contradiction to the main idea in the Declaration of Independence: "All men are created equal." To be a slave in the South meant being less than human; it meant being no more than property. As new states joined the Union, the question of slavery caused more and more tension.

When civil war finally broke out in 1861, the citizens of Fredericksburg—a small, thriving port in Northern Virginia—probably didn't realize how strategically placed their town was and how the war would ravage it and the surrounding countryside. One of the worst battles in the war occurred in Fredericksburg in December 1862, when the opposing armies fought in the very streets where the townspeople lived and worked. To the white people of Fredericksburg the Union Army was a tornado blasting their town, but to the enslaved blacks it was the wind of liberty, blowing them into a free, if uncertain, future. This book is the story of Fredericksburg, the war, and the people on all sides who fought and lived it.

The families of soldiers often mailed them boxes full of cakes, fruit preserves, knitted socks, writing materials, newspapers, and other treats from home.

CHAPTER 1

A THRIVING PORT

After its founding in 1728, Fredericksburg became a thriving port town and cultural center in Northern Virginia.

GREAT
BAR...NS
H...
C...

ON ITS COURSE through Northern Virginia, the Rappahannock River tumbles from the heights of the Blue Ridge Mountains and flows downhill all the way to the Chesapeake Bay. About midway along its path, it trips over falls, making it impossible for larger boats to get any farther upstream. It's here at the fall line of the Rappahannock that the town of Fredericksburg grew up.

Its first streets were laid out along the river in 1728, and it soon became a bustling colonial port and the gateway to the western wilderness that lay beyond it. Wharves lined its riverfront, and ships carrying goods from Europe and the West Indies docked here, leaving with their hulls full of tobacco from nearby plantations, iron ore, timber, or farm products.

About ten years after Fredericksburg was founded, a young boy named George Washington moved with his family to a farm just across the river from Fredericksburg. He went to school in the town and spent much of his boyhood there. Later, his sister, Betty, would become a wealthy and respected woman in the area. She and her husband lived in the elegant manor house of one of the large plantations that dotted the fertile Rappahannock Valley. Like most Virginia planters, they owed their wealth in many ways to the slaves who worked their fields.

ABOUT TEN YEARS AFTER FREDERICKSBURG WAS FOUNDED, A YOUNG BOY NAMED **GEORGE WASHINGTON** MOVED WITH HIS FAMILY TO A FARM JUST ACROSS THE RIVER . . .

For enslaved Virginians, Fredericksburg's prosperity didn't mean a better life. They "belonged" to their masters and lived and worked according to their owners' whims. But as the 1800s began, more and more white Americans came to believe that slavery was wrong. Fredericksburg's white citizens had mixed ideas about slavery. They had grown up with it, and for better or worse, it was woven into their daily lives. Slaves worked in their masters' factories, farms, homes, hotels, and shops. Slavery made the white citizens' way of life possible and helped fuel their economy. The idea of abolishing slavery frightened or angered many of them, even though there were a few free black men and women who lived peacefully and productively in Fredericksburg and often did the same kind of work as the enslaved townspeople. Some were blacksmiths and others were barbers or wagon drivers. They were not considered equal to whites, but they still enjoyed that precious state of being free.

There were also a few white townspeople who wanted to abolish slavery. One of them, Mary Minor Blackford, wrote, "Think of what it is to be a slave!!! To be treated not as a man but as . . . a thing to be bought and sold, to have no rights to the fruits of your own labour, no rights to your own wife or children."

Mrs. Blackford supported a plan known as colonization, which involved freeing slaves and resettling them outside the U.S. In 1821 to 1822, the West African nation of Liberia, whose name echoes liberty, was founded for just that purpose, and some of Fredericksburg's freed blacks emigrated there. Still, the black people of the town—and the nation—were as American as their white neighbors. Most didn't want to be uprooted and shipped across the Atlantic to West Africa. In fact, when the owner of Chatham, one of the largest plantations in the Fredericksburg area, freed 92 of her slaves in her will, she gave them the choice of moving to Liberia or becoming the property of one of her relatives. Most chose to stay in Virginia, and the state courts denied the others the right to leave.

The slavery question loomed larger and larger as new states joined the young American nation. Should they be admitted as slave states or free states? Tempers in Congress flared whenever this prickly subject was debated. Then in 1820—in fact, while one of Fredericksburg's former citizens, James Monroe,

A wooden canteen hand-decorated with the "stars and bars," the first official Confederate flag. Union soldiers carried bigger tin canteens that didn't leak as much.

THERE WERE ALSO A FEW
WHITE TOWNSPEOPLE
WHO WANTED TO
ABOLISH SLAVERY.

was fifth President of the U.S.—a compromise was struck. For every free state admitted, a slave state would also be admitted to the United States. For about 40 years, the Missouri Compromise, as it was known, maintained an uneasy peace between the abolitionist and proslavery factions.

Despite these simmering national tensions, Fredericksburg continued to prosper, particularly after the opening of the Richmond, Fredericksburg, and Potomac Railroad, which connected Fredericksburg to the Virginia capital of Richmond in the south and to the national capital of Washington in the north. The RF&P's slogan was "Linking North & South." But Fredericksburg's strategic location between the North and the South would soon turn from an advantage to a curse.

"At about 4 years of age mother learned me the alphabet from the 'New York Primer'. I was kept at my lessons an hour or two each night by my mother . . ."

VOICE FROM THE PAST
JOHN WASHINGTON

I WAS BORN (in Fredericksburg, Virginia, May, 20th 1838) a slave. When I was about 2 years of age My Mother (who was also a slave) was hired to one Richard L. Brown in Orange County Virginia about 37 miles from Fredericksburg, and I was taken along with her . . .

My recollections of my early childhood has been no doubt the most pleasant of my life . . . playing mostly with the White children on the farm, in Summer's evening among the sweet scented cloverfields. Often at night singing and dancing Prayer Meetings or corn shucking . . .

At about 4 years of age mother learned me the alphabet from the "New York Primer". I was kept at my lessons an hour or two each night by my mother . . .

My first Great Sorrow was caused by seeing one morning, a number of the "Plantation Hands" formed into line, with little Bundles straped to their backs, Men Women and children, and all marched off to be sold South away from all that was near and dear to them . . . perhaps never to meet again on Earth . . .

Later in his life, former slave John Washington (played by a reenactor above) wrote about his childhood in the Virginia countryside.

Mother with me and four others . . . was sent to Fredericksburg, Va . . .

Poor Mother struggled hard late and early to get a poor pittance for the children all of which was too small to help her. I was kept at the house of the "Old Mistress," all day to run errands . . .

Mother lived alone and maintained us children for about 2 years, perhaps, when Mrs. Taliaferro came to the conclusion that Mother, With my Sisters, Lousia, Laura, Georgianna, and brother Willie would have to be sent to Staunton Virginia, to be hired to one R. H. Phillips . . .

The night before Mother left me . . . her tears mingled with mine amid kisses and heart felt sorrow . . .

Bitter pangs filled my heart and I thought I would rather die . . .

Then and there My hatred was kindled secretly against my oppressors and I promised myself if ever I got an opportunity I would run away from the devilish Slave holders.

This is an excerpt from the memoirs of an enslaved Virginian named John Washington.

CHAPTER 2

A NATION AT WAR

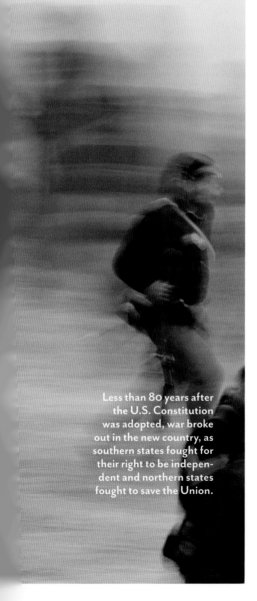

Less than 80 years after the U.S. Constitution was adopted, war broke out in the new country, as southern states fought for their right to be independent and northern states fought to save the Union.

THE COLD WIND OF EARLY MARCH blew through Washington, D.C., in 1861 as a tall, thin man in a stovepipe hat stood in front of the Capitol. He was about to take the oath of office as 16th President of the United States. The problem was, the states in the new nation, less than a century old, were no longer united. Since Abraham Lincoln had been elected in November, seven southern states had left the Union because their people believed this man from the North would abolish slavery. They had formed the Confederate States of America and had elected their own president, Jefferson Davis. In Lincoln's inaugural address, he told the nation that he had no plans to abolish slavery, but he also said that the Union would "constitutionally defend, and maintain itself."

A month later, it had to do just that. Southern forces fired on U.S. troops in Fort Sumter, South Carolina, and their shots echoed through the country. Four more southern states seceded, including Virginia, the most populated and industrialized state in the South. Richmond, Virginia's capital, was soon declared the capital of the Confederacy. Fredericksburg lay just 50 miles north of it—and 50 miles south of Washington. Throughout the town, people watched and waited for word as armies began to form and war filled the air.

Most of the town's 3,300 white citizens hoped that their new nation, the Confederate States, would win this conflict and continue the old way of life, dependent on slavery. But

Decorative detail from Union soldier's gear

SINCE ABRAHAM LINCOLN HAD BEEN ELECTED PRESIDENT,
7 SOUTHERN STATES
HAD LEFT THE UNION . . .

many of the enslaved townsfolk—and there were about 1,300 of them—secretly wished for a northern victory. They hoped that sooner or later, it would mean some kind of freedom for them.

In Hampton, Virginia, at the edge of the Chesapeake Bay, the North had managed to hold on to Fort Monroe. When three slaves escaped there, the officer in control of the fort, Benjamin Butler, refused to return them to their Confederate masters. Butler said that the black men were the "contraband of war." This was a big step, because the United States still had the Fugitive Slave Act, which declared that runaway slaves had to be returned. When word about Butler's decision spread, hundreds of slaves risked their lives to reach Fort Freedom, as they called Fort Monroe.

TO THE NATION'S AMAZEMENT— AND LINCOLN'S DISMAY—THE

NORTH LOST

AT MANASSAS.

In both the North and the South, the white people were clamoring for battle, and in July 1861, they got what they wanted. On the hills and fields along Bull Run Creek, near the railroad junction of Manassas, Virginia, and not far from Fredericksburg, the two great armies finally faced off. The Northerners were so sure of victory that families from Washington, 30 miles away, had driven out with picnic baskets to watch the Southerners be defeated. But war is never predictable, or entertaining. To the nation's amazement—and Lincoln's dismay—the North lost at Manassas. An English reporter described the retreating Union soldiers this way: "Faces black and dusty, tongues out in the heat, eyes staring—it was a most wonderful sight." The North, much more powerful and wealthier than the South, had lost the first major battle of the Civil War.

Lincoln pushed his generals to be more aggressive, and they fought battles in the West, along the Mississippi River, all through the next winter. In Fredericksburg the citizens were fighting a different kind of war—against disease. In September scarlet fever had taken its first

TOP RIGHT— A relieved wife greets her Confederate soldier husband after the First Battle of Bull Run. A year later, in the summer of 1862, the armies would be back, fighting for the same ground again.

BOTTOM RIGHT— The first battle of the war, along Bull Run Creek, was the bloodiest so far in America's short history, with close to 5,000 casualties. But in the next four years of war, there would be many, far bloodier battles ahead.

victim, and it targeted children as it swept through the town. Today's doctors use antibiotics to treat scarlet fever—which is basically strep throat plus a whole-body rash—but in the 1800s it was deadly. The epidemic raged for more than a year and took many children's lives in Fredericksburg.

IN SPRING 1862, military war began to rage again in Virginia. Off Fort Monroe, there was a battle unlike any fought before. Two ships covered in iron plates, one Union and one Confederate, challenged each other. There was no clear winner in the Battle of the Ironclads, but soon after that, Fort Monroe bustled with Union troops, as thousands of

soldiers landed to begin a march on Richmond, some 70 miles away.

Throughout the spring and summer, battles erupted across Virginia. The North's army got close to the Confederate capital, but it never managed to take Richmond and bring the war to an end. Finally, in in August, the Union Army was ordered north again.

When the campaign against Richmond had first begun, almost 30,000 troops had marched south from the Washington area toward Richmond. But they never got that far. On May 2, 1862, they threw floating pontoon bridges into the Rappahannock, crossed the river into Fredericksburg, and peacefully took possession of the town. The southern troops in the area had fled

TOP—
With Union troops occupying their town, these women take time to pray for their friends and families in the local Presbyterian church.

RIGHT—
The Union Army used floating pontoon bridges to cross the Rappahannock River and reach Fredericksburg, on the other side.

THE WOMEN, HE SAID,
"ARE RILING MAD AND CAN'T HELP
SHOWING THEIR DISLIKE AND
HATRED

TO THE UNION SOLDIERS.

Townswomen in Fredericksburg were often rude and defiant to the Northerners who occupied their town in the spring and summer of 1862.

before them and had burned bridges and cargo ships on the river to keep them out of enemy hands.

A northern soldier named Alf wrote a long letter describing the occupation of Fredericksburg. The women, he said, "are riling mad and can't help showing their dislike and hatred" to the Union soldiers. "The majority of the Fredericksburg merchants have 'vamoosed their ranches,' some for the purpose of joining the rebel army and others for fear the 'Yanks' would kill them . . ." Northern peddlers following the army took their place because, as Alf wrote, "so long as the army continues in this vicinity there will be a brisk retail trade as soldiers, like sailors, will spend their small change for knicknacks whether they want them or not." Alf also wrote that it was "a sight to see the hundreds of slaves making tracks . . . The great exodus of these people from the land of gloom into the free States is truly remarkable."

All in all, as Alf wrote, the occupation was "a hard pill" for the townspeople to swallow, to see "the might of our men parading their streets after all their vain boastings that no Yankee soldiers should ever walk the streets of Fredericksburg alive while the chivalrous soldiers of Virginia held possession of the city. Can't be helped, poor Old Virginia, you must grin and bear it until you return to your allegiance and again pay homage to the Old Flag."

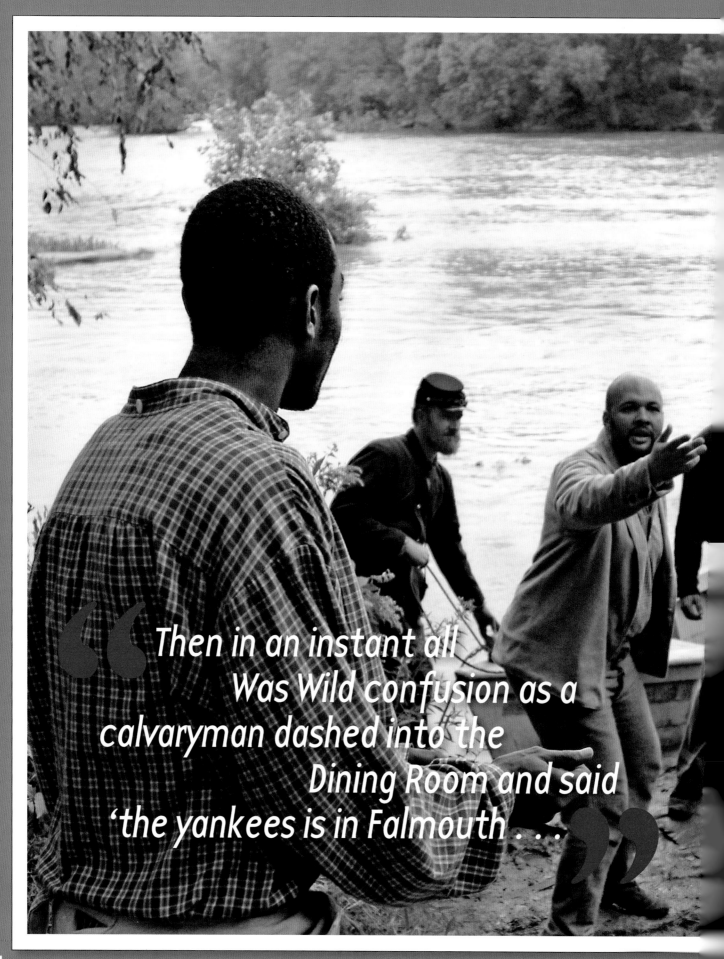

"Then in an instant all
Was Wild confusion as a
calvaryman dashed into the
Dining Room and said
'the yankees is in Falmouth . . . "

VOICE FROM THE PAST
JOHN WASHINGTON

APRIL 18TH, 1862. Was "Good-Friday," the Day was a mild pleasant one with the Sun Shining brightly, and every thing unusally quite, the Hotel was crowed with boarders who was Seated at breakfast A rumor had been circulated amoung them that the yankees was advancing. but nobody Seemed to beleive it, until every body Was Startled by Several reports of cannon.

Then in an instant all Was Wild confusion as a calvaryman dashed into the Dining Room and said "the yankees is in Falmouth . . ."

In less time than it takes me to write these lines, every White man was out the house. Every Man Servant was out on the house top looking over the River at the yankees for their glistening bayonats could eaziely be Seen I could not begin to express my new born hopes for I felt already like I Was certain of My freedom now . . .

We left the road just before we got to "Ficklin's Mill," and walked down to the river . . .

Very Soon one of a party of Soilders, in a boat call out to the crowd Standing arround me do any of you want to come over—Every body "Said no"—I hallowed out, "Yes, I Want to come over," "All right—Bully for you" was the response. and, they was soon over to Our Side. I greeted them gladly and Stepped into their Boat . . .

After we had landed on the other Side, a large crowd of the Soilders off duty, gathered around Us and asked all kinds of questions in reference to the Whereabouts of the "Rebels" I had Stuffed My pockets full of rebel newspapers and, I distributed them around as far as they would go greatly to the delight of the men . . ."Said Several at once" the District of Columbia is free now. Emancapated 2 Days ago. I did not know What to Say for I Was dumb With Joy and could only thank God and Laugh.

---❖---

This description of the Union Army's arrival in Fredericksburg is also from John Washington's memoir. Washington served as a cook and aid to Union general Rufus King. After the war, he and his wife, Annie, moved to Washington, D.C., and had four sons.

CHAPTER 3

THE ONGOING FIGHT

An officer salutes troops on guard at Chatham, a fine old manor the Union Army commandeered for its 1862 headquarters. Across the river from Fredericksburg, it had good views of the town and riverfront.

ALL THROUGH THE SPRING AND SUMMER of 1862,

the streets of Fredericksburg swarmed with the Union troops occupying the area. Their commander, General McDowell, had taken over the old Chatham manor house, on a hill above the Rappahannock. It had a good view of the city across the river, and from this perch, the general could oversee the repair of the RF&P Railroad and the construction of new bridges across the river. President Lincoln had come to Chatham in the spring to meet with the general. A town newspaper reported that he "rode in a carriage drawn by four fine iron-gray horses. They crossed the Rappahannock River on the canal-boat bridge . . . There were no demonstrations of joy, however, from any citizens."

The Union troops stayed in Fredericksburg for five months. During that time, more and more of the enslaved people of the town realized they didn't have to let their owners control them. In fact, they didn't even have to stay with their masters. Floods of African Americans escaped to the town, and this added to the discomfort of the white citizens. "The negroes are going off in great numbers, and beginning to be very independent and impertinent," Mrs. Betty Maury wrote in her diary. "We hear that our three are going soon. I am afraid of the lawless Yankee soldiers, but that is nothing to my fear of the negroes if they should rise against us."

"I AM AFRAID OF THE LAWLESS YANKEE SOLDIERS BUT THAT IS NOTHING TO MY FEAR OF THE NEGROES IF THEY SHOULD RISE AGAINST US."

In a strange twist of history, at the end of August 1862, the great armies of the North and the South met on the same ground they had fought on over a year earlier—along Bull Run Creek not far from Fredericksburg. Now seasoned in battle, they fought longer and harder this time, but again the North lost. The war in Virginia was going badly for the United States and for Lincoln's cause—to reunite the country.

Days after their victory at Bull Run, the southern Army, under Robert E.

With the Union Army in the area, many slaves left their white masters and claimed their freedom.

Lee, crossed the Potomac River into Maryland. It was the South's first invasion of the North, and it was a bold move. "The men are poorly provided with clothes and in thousands of instances are destitute of shoes," Lee told Confederate president, Jefferson Davis. "Still we cannot afford to be idle, and though weaker than our opponents in men and military equipments, must endeavor to harass, if we cannot destroy them."

The Union Army was soon on Lee's trail, with twice as many men as he had. But as usual, they moved slowly and cautiously and let Lee get ahead of them. Then, on September 13, they got lucky. Soldiers strolling through an abandoned Confederate campground found a copy of Lee's orders to his other commanders wrapped around some cigars. Lee's forces were smaller than the Union general George McClellan had thought, and they were divided and vulnerable. McClellan pushed his men forward. Lincoln sent him a telegraph saying, "God bless you, and all with you . . . Destroy the rebel army, if possible."

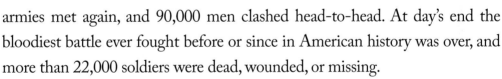

At dawn on September 17, again along a creek—this time called Antietam—the armies met again, and 90,000 men clashed head-to-head. At day's end the bloodiest battle ever fought before or since in American history was over, and more than 22,000 soldiers were dead, wounded, or missing.

A young woman named Clara Barton, one of the medical volunteers who followed the Union army, helped treat the wounded at Antietam. "Oh! God what a costly war," she wrote. She described removing an enemy ball from one soldier's jaw: "This man could laugh at pain, face death without a tremor, and yet weep like a child over the loss of his comrades and his captain."

General McClellan had dealt a deadly blow to Lee's army, but he did not destroy it, as Lincoln had urged. For some reason, he let Lee and his soldiers limp back into Virginia. Still, the North declared Antietam a victory. With good news at last, Lincoln took the opportunity to do something momentous and controversial, even for many Northerners. He issued the Emancipation Proclamation: As of January 1863 all slaves in the southern states in rebellion "shall be then, thenceforward, and forever free."

RIGHT—
Clara Barton (reenactor), one of the volunteers who followed the Union Army to care for the sick and wounded, later founded the American Red Cross.

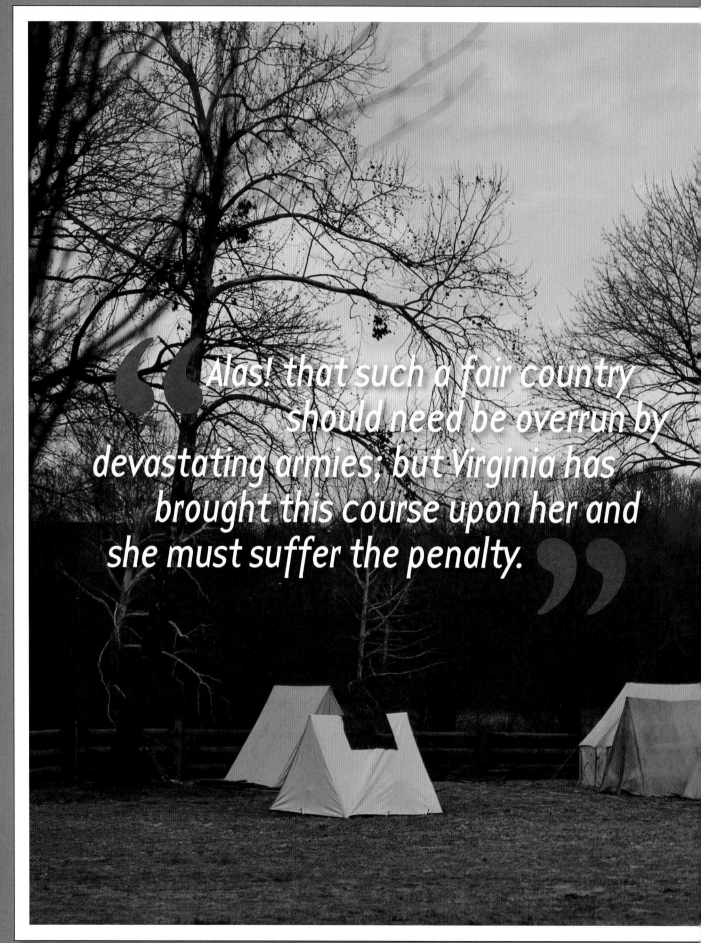

"Alas! that such a fair country should need be overrun by devastating armies; but Virginia has brought this course upon her and she must suffer the penalty."

UNION SOLDIER

TWO WEEKS AGO last night I arrived at the camp of my regiment on the banks of the Rappahannock and this morning's sun found us still upon that clover-carpeted hill overlooking the city of Fredericksburg on the opposite shore of the river, and the beautiful valley through which the Rappahannock winds its course to the sea . . .

Our brigade had the railroad bridge to build and part of each regiment was detailed for that purpose while the remainder drilled some, did some guard duty, and the rest of their time they amused themselves by pitching quoits, (a favorite sport of the Greek soldiers at the siege of Troy,) playing chess, chequers, and a variety of games with cards, besides reading all the papers and books they could get and manufacturing news when the papers failed to furnish a sufficient supply . . . We crossed the Rappahannock on a bridge of boats, an ancient, but an excellent way of bridging a river . . .

We took a road leading nearly south and through the loveliest part of Virginia that I have yet seen. True, it bears the marks of war. The fences in many places are destroyed and but few white persons are to be seen, but a more beautiful country than the valley of the Rappahannock can seldom be found either East or West. The road is a good substantial turnpike, lined on either side by cedar trees that grow so close together in some places as to form a complete fence, and stretching away as far as the eye can reach are large prairie-like fields, covered with luxuriant growth of clover in blossom, wheat and rye in head, or corn that looks yellow and sickly seeming entirely behind the season. These fields are interspersed with woody hills that look like Islands in the ocean. Alas! that such a fair country should need be overrun by devastating armies; but Virginia has brought this course upon her and she must suffer the penalty.

Camp life during the occupation of Fredericksburg, as described by a soldier in the Second Wisconsin, his name lost to history

CHAPTER 4

WAR HAS
COME

As Union guns pound Fredericksburg, Confederate soldiers help townsfolk flee to safer ground.

RIGHT—
A recruiting poster for the Irish Brigade, famous for its valor at the Battle of Fredericksburg.

AFTER ANTIETAM, Lincoln asked one of the heroes of the battle, Ambrose Burnside, to take over as commander of the Union forces in Virginia. Burnside didn't think he was the right man for the job, but he agreed to take it.

Right away, Burnside started planning another attack on Richmond. This time the Union Army would march overland from the North. They would have to cross several rivers along the way, and the first was the Rappahannock. The army would use floating pontoon bridges to do that.

Burnside moved fast, and by mid-November 1862 about 110,000 Union troops were across the river from Fredericksburg and encamped around the town of Falmouth. Burnside was ready to cross the Rappahannock and march "On to Richmond!"

But that didn't happen. The pontoon bridges he had ordered arrived weeks late, and in that time Robert E. Lee began gathering his own forces on the Fredericksburg side of the river.

On November 20, a Union soldier wrote, "The enemy occupy the range of hills opposite, and are working night and day to make them impregnable ... No better position for defense could be found, and Lee must thank his stars Burnside did not establish himself on the side when he had a chance to do so almost unopposed. It is strange how constantly we fall short in our endeavors at the very moment when we might succeed."

That same day the mayor of Fredericksburg was presented with an official letter from a Union general who demanded "a surrender of the city into my hands."

BURNSIDE MOVED FAST, AND BY MID-NOVEMBER 1862 ABOUT **110,000** UNION TROOPS WERE ACROSS THE RIVER FROM FREDERICKSBURG ...

If the city refused, he wrote, the North would "proceed to shell the town." The city did refuse, but the North had also promised to wait 16 hours so that "women and children, the sick, wounded and aged" could leave. Most left "as fast as possible," with the help of the Confederate Army. "Our ambulances have been running all day, and are now going back and forth, carrying out families," one general wrote. General Lee himself wrote on November 22, "I was moving out the women & children all last night & today. It was a piteous sight. But they have brave hearts. What is to become of them God only knows."

Some stayed with friends and relatives in nearby farms or towns. Others crowded into churches, hotels, and other buildings, where they slept on floors and huddled by strangers. Some slept in abandoned slave cabins or had to camp out in the woods, and they tried to find warmth in the cold, damp days of late autumn. They had no idea when, or whether, they would ever be able to return to their homes in Fredericksburg.

Lee's own soldiers suffered, too. Their tattered clothes and bare feet made the winter chill even worse. And they were often hungry. Armies eat vast amounts of food, and the many soldiers who had marched back and forth across Virginia since the war began had exhausted food supplies. Also, with so many men living together and with little means of keeping clean, diseases—

malaria, typhoid, measles, mumps, and diarrhea—struck often and could sweep through camps on both sides. Still, Lee's men trusted him to see them through the battle to come.

Burnside's own commanders were more worried. The pontoons had finally arrived, and the general had a new plan of battle. His army would cross the river at Fredericksburg, on three different pontoon bridges. He hoped he could divide Lee's forces that way, but it was a huge risk.

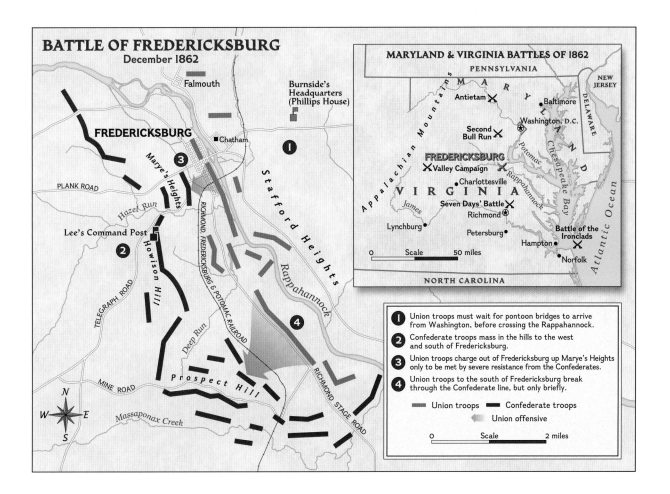

BATTLE OF FREDERICKSBURG
December 1862

Falmouth

Burnside's Headquarters (Phillips House)

FREDERICKSBURG

Chatham

3 Marye's Heights

PLANK ROAD

Hazel Run

Lee's Command Post

2

Howison Hill

TELEGRAPH ROAD

RICHMOND, FREDERICKSBURG & POTOMAC RAILROAD

Deep Run

Stafford Heights

Rappahannock

1

4

Prospect Hill

MINE ROAD

RICHMOND STAGE ROAD

Massaponax Creek

N W E S

MARYLAND & VIRGINIA BATTLES OF 1862

PENNSYLVANIA

NEW JERSEY

MARYLAND

Antietam ✗

Baltimore

Washington, D.C.

DELAWARE

Second Bull Run ✗

FREDERICKSBURG

Valley Campaign ✗

Charlottesville

VIRGINIA

Seven Days' Battle ✗

Richmond ⊛

Potomac

Rappahannock

Chesapeake Bay

Appalachian Mountains

James

Lynchburg

Petersburg

Battle of the Ironclads ✗

Hampton

Norfolk

Atlantic Ocean

Scale 50 miles

NORTH CAROLINA

1 Union troops must wait for pontoon bridges to arrive from Washington, before crossing the Rappahannock.

2 Confederate troops mass in the hills to the west and south of Fredericksburg.

3 Union troops charge out of Fredericksburg up Marye's Heights only to be met by severe resistance from the Confederates.

4 Union troops to the south of Fredericksburg break through the Confederate line, but only briefly.

▬ Union troops ▬ Confederate troops

Union offensive

0 Scale 2 miles

On December 9 Union soldiers were ordered to put 60 rounds of ammunition and three days' worth of cooked rations in their haversacks and be ready to march at any time. The men may have been afraid, but most put on hearty, confident faces. One New Jersey man admitted, "I hope that come what will it will never be said I was a coward." A Pennsylvania sergeant was more blunt: "'On to Richmond' has prevailed over reason and we must go! Well, go we will, but not without apprehension. Those terrible heights before us are enough to terrify, but we will do our best . . ."

As darkness deepened on the night of December 10, the pontoon boats, loaded on almost 200 wagons, were moved to the river. Men wrestled the pontoons off the wagons and carried them down a steep bank to the river. Hooking the pontoons together to form a bridge was hard work, but the pontooniers worked fast. They expected to hear gunfire at any minute, but the other side was "still as death."

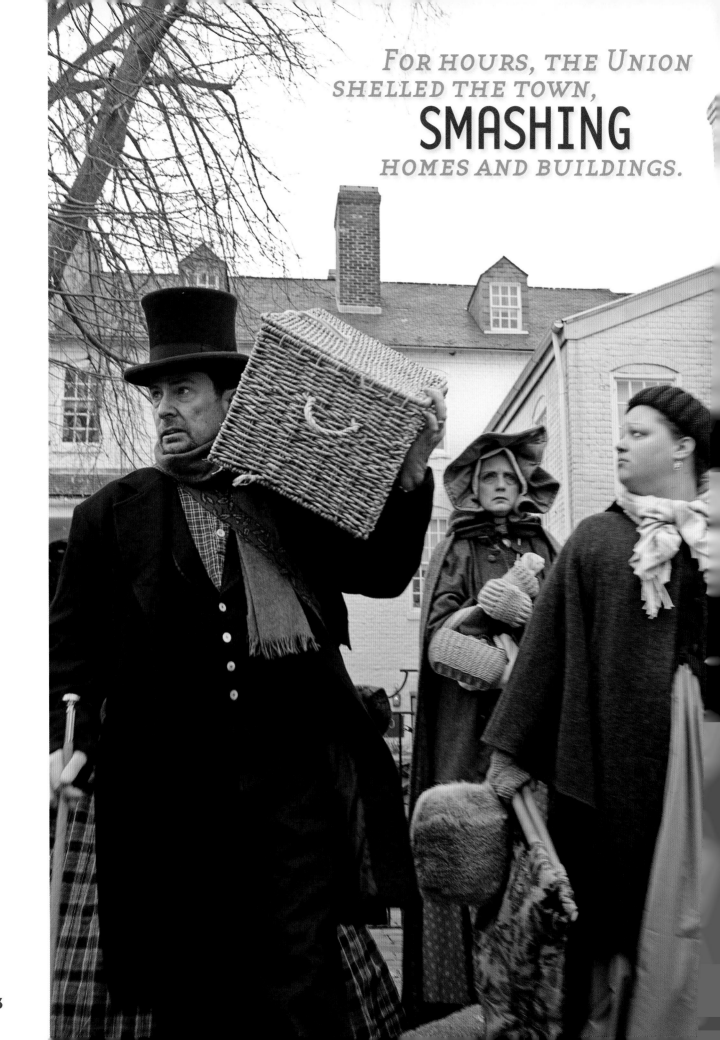

FOR HOURS, THE UNION SHELLED THE TOWN, **SMASHING** HOMES AND BUILDINGS.

When dawn finally arrived, a heavy mist made it hard to see. But "as the fogg lifted for a little," one of the pontoon captains wrote, "I saw, what for the moment almost chilled my blood." The muskets of Confederate troops lined the riverfront in Fredericksburg! Soon "the bulletts of the enemy ... went whizzing and spitting by and around me." The "deep thunder" of northern cannon answered the fire, and the ground shook with the blasts. The battle had begun.

For hours, the Union shelled the town, smashing homes and buildings. "Flash succeeded flash, leaping like light-ning from the cannon's mouth, a solid mass of flames ... a heavy crashing thunder roll-ing over the valley, and up the hills," wrote a Union chaplain. Any townspeople who had stayed in their homes ran to their basements and huddled together. As the day went on, Union soldiers managed to cross the pontoon bridges and enter the town, where the fight-ing went on, sometimes house to house. That

night, more "women and children crowded the public roads, fleeing from their desolate homes. The weather was extremely cold—the mud on the highway six inches deep—the roads filled with frozen clods of earth. It was heart-rending to hear the weeping of these fugitives," a southern soldier wrote.

By December 12, the Union had taken over the smoking, shattered ruins of Fredericksburg. Then, setting about to destroy what was left, they looted houses and shops of food, drink, tobacco, and belongings. The war had been hard, but for that night, "Oh we lived like kings," one soldier said. Another admitted, "Our men took what they chose, and destroyed any amount of prop-erty of all kinds." Yet another wrote sadly, "The citizens of Fredericksburg are houseless, Homeless and destitute."

Even in the midst of their wild looting, the men knew what lay ahead the next day, when the fighting would begin again. The enemy held the high ground. Many of them would die charging across the open plain beyond town to reach Lee's army.

LEFT—
After the Union bombardment ends, civilians still in town pack up the few possessions they can carry and leave their homes behind.

RIGHT—
The night of December 12, northern soldiers ransack homes and businesses all over town.

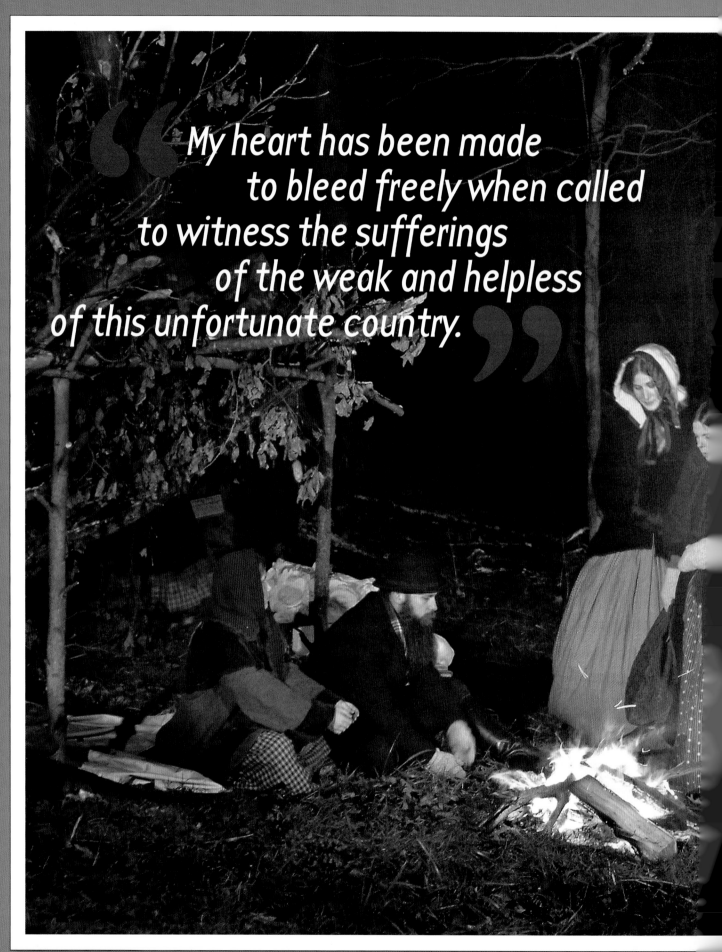

"My heart has been made to bleed freely when called to witness the sufferings of the weak and helpless of this unfortunate country."

VOICE FROM THE PAST
JANE BEALE

AS WE PASSED beyond the line of the town and the turn of the road put the 'Willis Hill' Promontory of land, between us and the firing, a sense of security came into my mind. Crowds of women and children had sought refuge in this sheltered spot and as night drew on they were in great distress, they could not return to the town which was already in possession of the enemy, and they had fled too hastily to bring with them the comforts even the necessaries of life. Some few had stretched blue yarn counterpanes or pieces of old carpet over sticks, stuck in the ground—and the little ones were huddled together under these tents, the women were weeping the children crying loudly, I saw one walking along with a baby in her arms and another little one not three years old clinging to her dress and crying "I want to go home" My heart ached for them . . .

Fredericksburg is almost depopulated. The few that remain in town after the first days excitement continue to leave. Wagons loaded with furniture pass our camp constantly. The women and children have been removed to the country. Where they find shelter from the wind and the rain I cannot tell, but as far as I can learn every farm house is filled to repletion . . . Virginia is truly unfortunate in being the theater upon which this monster war is enacted. Those of our citizens far removed from the seat of war cannot understand how thankful they should be. My heart has been made to bleed freely when called to witness the sufferings of the weak and helpless inhabitants of this unfortunate country.

Jane Beale, who had stayed in Fredericksburg with her family, finally fled on December 11. She wrote this description of what she saw as she left town.

CONCLUSION

The next day, December 13, the Union soldiers crossing the open plain below Marye's Heights were mowed down by Confederate fire over and over again, but they kept coming.

A newspaper reporter watching the battle wrote, "It can hardly be in human nature for men to show more valor or generals to manifest less judgment." To the south of town there was more fierce fighting, and at one point, the North actually broke through Stonewall Jackson's lines on Prospect Hill. It was the only victory the North had all day—and it was soon over.

Men prayed that the day— and with it, the fighting—would be over. When the sun set and a cold wind blew the night in, the guns were finally quiet. "The wounded lay everywhere about us, and to assist the stretcher-bearers in finding them quickly, these poor fellows were told by their comrades to groan continually," a Union soldier reported. In all, 13,000 Union soldiers were dead or wounded to the South's 5,000. And yet, Burnside wasn't ready to quit. He wanted to lead another charge against the Rebels the next day himself, but his officers wouldn't support the idea.

The people of Fredericksburg had lost their town, and the North had suffered a catastrophic defeat. In Washington, news of the battle devastated Lincoln. "If there is a worse place than Hell," he said, "I am in it."

After the Union defeat at Fredericksburg, fierce fighting went on and on all through Virginia, until the long, bloody war finally ended in 1865.

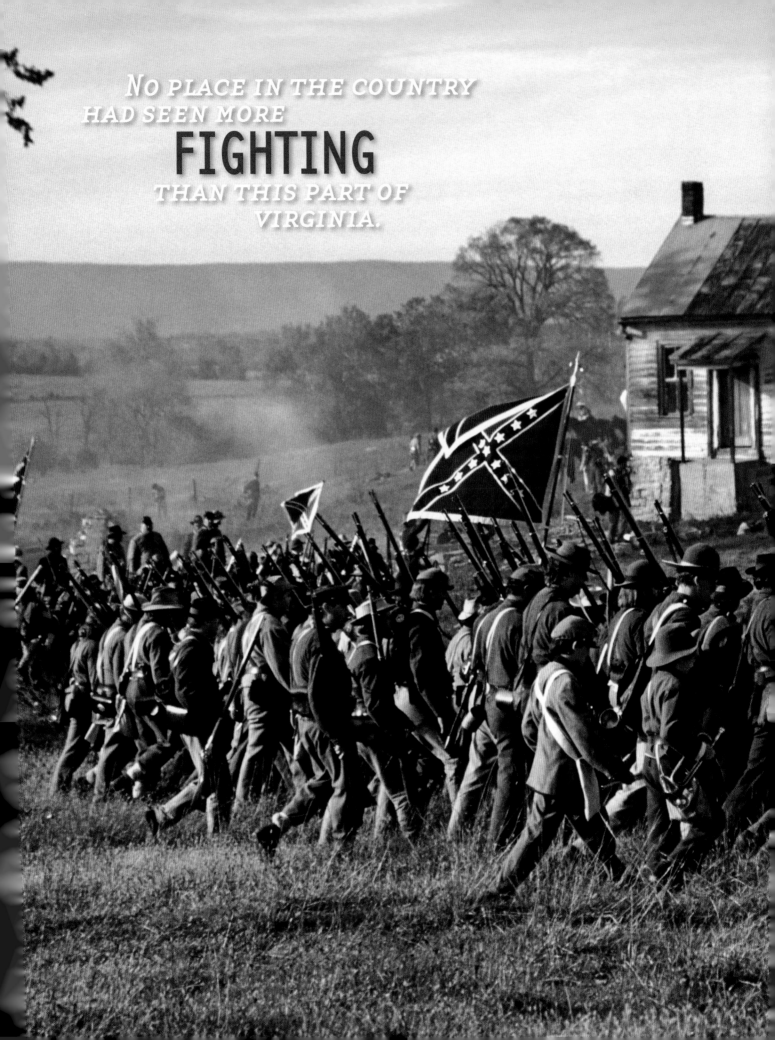

No place in the country had seen more **FIGHTING** than this part of Virginia.

His political enemies used the defeat against him, and there were rumors that he and his cabinet would resign. Americans now understood that this would be a long, terrible war. Some Northerners even wanted to end it and let the Confederacy stand as its own nation.

But Lincoln would not let the Union die, and on January 20, Burnside's army was on the march again, with plans to cross the Rappahannock above Fredericksburg. This time, his men battled against rain and sleet that bogged them down on muddy roads. After three days of the so-called Mud March, Burnside called it off. For the winter, the fighting stopped in Virginia.

Yet the area around Fredericksburg had not seen the end of battle. More than two years of war lay ahead, and the armies of the North and the South kept returning to the region—once the following spring of 1863 for the Battle of Chancellorsville and again a year later, for the awful Battles of the Wilderness and Spotsylvania Court House. When the armies moved on for the last time in May 1864, the land around Fredericksburg was treeless, the food gone, the ground soaked with blood. No place in the country had seen more fighting than this part of Virginia.

The next spring, 1865, Lee finally surrendered. A few days later, Lincoln was assassinated, but he died knowing that the Union he loved had been preserved, and not a man, woman, or child would ever again be a slave in the United States.

For white Virginians, the war and the Confederate defeat shattered their lives, their homes, and their future. One former planter in the Fredericksburg area said, "We are a ruined people . . . The whole of the state is worth not one cent to any of us."

LEFT— During the Battle of Fredericksburg, thousands of Union soldiers died charging Marye's Heights. Today a national cemetery occupies this high ground.

RIGHT— The wrapper from a box of Confederate rifle bullets. Rifles were the latest technology in weapons of death during the war. They could shoot farther and more accurately than the old muskets.

RIFLE MUSKET & RIFLE 58
71 GRAINS M. POWDER
FRANKFORD ARSENAL
1863

BRINGING THE PAST TO LIFE

It took Fredericksburg many decades to rebuild itself and to regain its dignity after the Civil War was over. So many of the buildings had been destroyed, but miraculously three churches had survived, and their steeples were like beacons of hope. Many of the townspeople gradually returned, and by the end of the 1800s a few new industries had come to town. They were followed by more in the next century and by a new college for women named after George Washington's mother, Mary.

Even today, though, the scars—and memories—of war remain. Cannonballs and shell fragments can still be seen in the walls of some buildings, and the town's two major cemeteries are reminders of how terrible and costly war is. At the Fredericksburg Confederate Cemetery in town, six generals and some 3,300 Confederate soldiers are buried; more than 2,000 of them are unknown. Just a few blocks away, up on Marye's Heights, the nation established the Fredericksburg National Cemetery right after the war was over. Men buried on nearby battlefields and camps were moved here, and the cemetery now holds the graves of 15,000 Union soldiers; almost 13,000 of them are unknown. Many of them fell trying to take these very heights.

The national cemetery and many other sites are now preserved as part of the Fredericksburg and Spotsylvania National Military Park. The battlefields west of town at Chancellorsville, the Wilderness, and Spotsylvania Court House are also preserved. Chatham, the great manor house across the river, is part of the park as well. From its vantage point, you can see what the Union commanders saw as they looked out on Fredericksburg.

Today, the town is dedicated to remembering both its own history and the valor of the people who died in the Civil War. Museums tell the story of the war, while shops and galleries sell photographs and memorabilia related to it. And every year in mid-December, volunteers from all over the mid-Atlantic, both men and women, gather in Fredericksburg to reenact those long days of battle and to honor the people on both sides who lost their lives in America's bloodiest war.

Every December reenactors (opposite, top right) from all over the mid-Atlantic gather to re-create the Battle of Fredericksburg. They set up authentic camps (opposite right) that "civilians" can visit to learn what a soldier's life was like in the Civil War.

A SOLDIER PORTRAYING A SOLDIER

Greg Hillenbrand serves as a soldier on two fronts—as a Civil War reenactor with the 28th Massachusetts and as a hospital corpsman actively serving in the U.S. Navy. A few days after the reenactment of the 1862 Fredericksburg battle, he left for Afghanistan to serve his country in the ongoing war there. "I wanted to spend my last weekend with the 28th, because they've become my friends, and any chance to spend time with friends before I leave is something I seize upon," says Hillenbrand. He can still see remnants of the Civil War in modern military drills and ceremonies and even in some medical practices.

FALL 1860: Abraham Lincoln is elected President of the U.S.

WINTER 1861: Before Lincoln is inaugurated in March, seven states secede from the Union to form their own country, the Confederate States of America.

SPRING 1861: Confederates fire on Union troops in Fort Sumter, off Charleston, and the Civil War begins. Four more states leave the Union to join the Confederacy, and Richmond, Virginia, just 50 miles south of Fredericksburg, becomes the Confederate capital.

SUMMER 1861: The Battle of Bull Run (also called Manassas), the first major battle between the North and the South, is fought about 30 miles west of Washington, D.C., in July. The Union loses.

FALL AND WINTER 1861–62: More battles are fought in Kentucky, Missouri, and Tennessee. In March, two ironclad ships duel in the waters off Fort Monroe, Virginia. Neither the North nor the South wins.

SPRING–SUMMER 1862: Union troops occupy Fredericksburg for almost five months. The Union also lands troops at Fort Monroe and begins a march on Richmond, 75 miles away. All around Virginia the fighting is fierce until early August, when Lincoln recalls the Union Army. Richmond remains in Confederate hands. In August, the Second Battle of Bull Run is another Union loss. In early September, Lee invades the North and the worst battle ever fought by Americans takes place at Antietam on September 17. The Union claims victory but allows Lee's army to retreat.

FALL 1862: Lincoln issues the preliminary Emancipation Proclamation, freeing slaves in the Confederate States. In November, Ambrose Burnside becomes head of the Union Army in Virginia and makes plans for a march on Richmond. His army of 110,000 marches to the banks of the Rappahannock, across from Fredericksburg. For five days in mid-December, a great battle consumes and destroys the town. The Union loses badly.

SPRING 1863: In May, the two armies meet again ten miles west of Fredericksburg at Chancellorsville, and the South scores another victory. In the West, the Union Army goes on the attack in Mississippi.

SUMMER 1863: The Battle of Gettysburg takes many lives, but the Union wins, marking a turning point in the war. Grant also takes the strategic port of Vicksburg, on the Mississippi. Fierce fighting continues, mostly in Tennessee.

FALL 1863: President Lincoln delivers his most famous speech, the Gettysburg Address.

WINTER 1864: Ulysses Grant takes over the Union Army in Virginia.

SPRING 1864: Grant marches into Virginia as he chases Lee's army. The first battles take place about 15 miles west of Fredericksburg, at the Wilderness, then at Spotsylvania Court House. The fighting between the two armies continues all spring.

SUMMER 1864: Lee's army digs in at Petersburg, Virginia, and Grant begins a siege of the town. In the Deep South, Sherman's Union Army is winning major battles and takes Atlanta, Georgia.

FALL 1864: Lincoln is reelected President. Sherman's army marches through Georgia and lays waste to everything in its path.

WINTER 1865: Sherman's troops move north and take more Confederate land. The U.S. Congress passes the 13th Amendment, outlawing slavery throughout the nation.

SPRING 1865: Grant forces Lee's army out of Petersburg. On April 9, Lee surrenders to Grant at Appomattox Court House, Virginia. Six days later, in Washington, Abraham Lincoln is assassinated. By late May all fighting is over, and Andrew Johnson is President of the reunited country.

BIBLIOGRAPHY

Abraham Lincoln's Extraordinary Era, by K. M. Kostyal, National Geographic, 2009.

Battle Cry of Freedom: The Civil War Era, by James McPherson, Ballantine Books, 1989.

Battles and Leaders of the Civil War: Retreat From Gettysburg, by Robert Underwood Johnson, Kessinger Publishing, 2004.

A Different Story: A Black History of Fredericksburg, Stafford and Spotsylvania, Virginia, by Ruth Coder Fitzgerald, Unicorn Press, 1979.

The Fredericksburg Campaign: Winter War on the Rappahannock, by Francis Augustín O'Reilly, Louisiana State University, 2006.

Fredericksburg! Fredericksburg! by George C. Rable, University of North Carolina Press, 2001.

Fredericksburg and Spotsylvania County Battlefields Memorial website, www.nps.gov/frsp/vc.htm

The History of The City of Fredericksburg, Virginia, by S.J. Quinn, Hermitage Press, 1908.

A Slave No More: Two Men Who Escaped to Freedom, Including Their Own Narratives of Emancipation, by David W. Blight, Houghton, Mifflin, Harcourt, 2007.

PRIMARY SOURCES

Abraham Lincoln's First Inaugural Address and The Emancipation Proclamation, both available through The Avalon Project: Documents in Law, History and Diplomacy, http://avalon.law.yale.edu

Letters written by men of the Second Wisconsin Regiment, available through the Second Wisconsin Volunteer Infantry website, www.secondwi.com/index.htm

Unpublished diaries of Jane Beale and Betty H. Maury

Johnny Reb and Billy Yank by Alexander Hunter, The Neale Publishing Company, 1905.

"The Shelling of Fredericksburg: Recollections of One Who Was a Little Girl at That Time," by Fanny Bernard, *Fredericksburg Daily Star,* December 6, 1909.

INDEX

To my ever valiant father —KMK

To my brothers Jon and Michael, who taught me how to fight fair —LE

Without the help of those dedicated to honoring the valor and suffering of the past, this book would not have been possible. In particular my thanks go to John Hennessy, Chief Historian at the Fredericksburg and Spotsylvania National Military Park, for his generous support, guidance, and expertise on this project, and to Rick Miller of Grey Ghost Gallery, who shared his knowledge and love of history and whose energy and perseverance make the annual battlefield reenactment possible. Also thanks to Sarah Poore and to Jerry Lynes and the other reenactors who battle cold, discomfort, and sometimes distance to bring the past to life. To my own small battle-hardened band of fellow bookmakers—Jennifer Emmett, Jim Hiscott, Lori Epstein, and Hillary Moloney. And a final, special acknowledgment to Greg Hillenbrand, who is fighting the current war in Afghanistan.

Published by the National Geographic Society

John M. Fahey, Jr., *Chairman of the Board and Chief Executive Officer*
Timothy T. Kelly, *President*
Declan Moore, *Executive Vice President; President, Publishing*
Melina Gerosa Bellows, *Executive Vice President; Chief Creative Officer, Books, Kids, and Family*

Prepared by the Book Division

Nancy Laties Feresten, *Senior Vice President, Editor in Chief, Children's Books*
Jonathan Halling, *Design Director, Books and Children's Publishing*
Jay Sumner, *Director of Photography, Children's Publishing*
Jennifer Emmett, *Editorial Director, Children's Books*
Carl Mehler, *Director of Maps*
R. Gary Colbert, *Production Director*
Jennifer A. Thornton, *Managing Editor*

Staff for This Book

Jennifer Emmett, *Project Editor*
James Hiscott, Jr., *Art Director/Designer*
Lori Epstein, *Senior Illustrations Editor*
Kate Olesin, *Editorial Assistant*
Kathryn Robbins, *Design Production Assistant*
Hillary Moloney, *Illustrations Assistant*
Grace Hill, *Associate Managing Editor*
Lewis R. Bassford, *Production Manager*
Susan Borke, *Legal and Business Affairs*

Manufacturing and Quality Management

Christopher A. Liedel, *Chief Financial Officer*
Phillip L. Schlosser, *Senior Vice President*
Chris Brown, *Technical Director*
Nicole Elliott, *Manager*
Rachel Faulise, *Manager*
Robert L. Barr, *Manager*

The National Geographic Society is one of the world's largest nonprofit scientific and educational organizations. Founded in 1888 to "increase and diffuse geographic knowledge," the Society works to inspire people to care about the planet. National Geographic reflects the world through its magazines, television programs, films, music and radio, books, DVDs, maps, exhibitions, live events, school publishing programs, interactive media, and merchandise. *National Geographic* magazine, the Society's official journal, published in English and 33 local-language editions, is read by more than 38 million people each month. The National Geographic Channel reaches 320 million households in 34 languages in 166 countries. National Geographic Digital Media receives more than 15 million visitors a month. National Geographic has funded more than 9,400 scientific research, conservation, and exploration projects and supports an education program promoting geography literacy. For more information, visit nationalgeographic.com.

For more information, please call 1-800-NGS LINE (647-5463) or write to the following address:
National Geographic Society
1145 17th Street N.W.
Washington, D.C. 20036-4688 U.S.A.

Visit us online at www.nationalgeographic.com/books
For librarians and teachers: www.ngchildrensbooks.org
More for kids from National Geographic: kids.nationalgeographic.com
For information about special discounts for bulk purchases, please contact National Geographic Books Special Sales: ngspecsales@ngs.org
For rights or permissions inquiries, please contact National Geographic Books Subsidiary Rights: ngbookrights@ngs.org

Library of Congress Cataloging-in-Publication Data
Kostyal, K. M., 1951-
1862, Fredericksburg : a new look at a bitter Civil War battle / by K.M. Kostyal.
   p. cm.
Includes index.
1. Fredericksburg, Battle of, Fredericksburg, Va., 1862—Juvenile literature. I. Title.
E474.85.K67 2011
973.7'336—dc22   2011011798

ISBN: 978-1-4263-0835-2 (hardcover)
ISBN: 978-1-4263-0836-9 (reinforced library binding)

Printed in China
11/RRDS/1